Is That What That Is

Paul Hostovsky

FUTURECYCLE PRESS
www.futurecycle.org

Cover art by Evelyn Goodstein; author photo by Jonathan O'Dell; cover and interior book design by Diane Kistner; Minion Pro text and ITC Avant Garde Gothic titling

Library of Congress Control Number: 2015939549

Published by FutureCycle Press
Athens, Georgia, USA

ISBN 978-1-942371-32-8

For Marlene. Always. Only.

Contents

If Only Life Were Like Language

and all the natural resources like words,
then the world would be
an unambiguously better place.
Because when you use a word
like *apocalypse,* say, it doesn't then follow
that there is one less apocalypse to go around—
there are still an infinite number of apocalypses,
more than enough for everyone. And the more
people who use a language the more
the language grows rich and strong
and resourceful and ramifying
with new and far-out ways of saying things,
not to mention all the lexical borrowings that go on,
the exotic words and phrases, and the names—
names of dinosaurs and flowers
and racehorses and hurricanes—
and the lists, praise be to God for the lists!
Which is just the opposite of the world
with its dying rivers and dwindling resources
and endangered species list.
With words you can make stuff up out of nothing
which is more than you can say
for physics or chemistry or corn. Earth's
the right place for language. I don't know where
else you could invent an imaginary escape hatch
up and out of a dying world,
and take a little of the world with you in your pockets,
like the jingling coins of a realm,
or like the crepitating bits and pieces
of a beautiful intact dead language
for sprinkling over the smart lunch conversation
in the next.

One Ambition

All I ever really wanted
was to whistle with my fingers—

I knew I would never
be the one up on stage

blowing everybody away
with beauty, brilliance, virtuosity...

But to be the lightning
inside the thunderous applause,

to have the audacity
and the manual dexterity

to make a siren screeching
through a dark auditorium,

to be the killer hawk
in all that parroting, pattering rain,

to be, finally, the very best at praise—
now that was something

I thought that if I gave my life to
I might attain.

The Calculus

My hygienist likes to include me
in the decision-making.
"Shall we use the hand scaler
or the ultrasonic today?" she asks me.
I like the way she says "we,"
like we're doing something intimate
and collaborative,
like building a snowman,
or more like dismantling one
after an ice storm, flake
by frozen flake. "The calculus
is caused by precipitation
of minerals from your saliva," she explains.
"You can't remove it with your toothbrush.
Only a professional can do that." She's very
professional. She doesn't dumb it down.
"Pay more attention to the lingual side
of your mandibular anteriors," she says.
I love it when she talks like that.
I love the names of teeth: incisor, third molar, bicuspid,
eyetooth. Her own teeth are
virtuosic. "*Calculus* comes from the Greek
for stone," she says. "In mathematics
it's counting with stones. In medicine,
it's the mineral buildup in the body: kidney stones,
tartar on teeth." She teaches me all this
as I sit there with my mouth open,
looking astonished.

Out of Place

When I see my dentist
in his baseball cap and sneakers
walking down the street like a regular guy

without a probe or excavator
or tiny round mirror in his hand,
no rubber gloves, no hygienist

sitting attentively across from him
anticipating his needs and my needs,
no tasteful prints on the wall,

no Muzak in the ceiling,
no adjustable overhead light—
just the sun shining down on both of us,

and him too far away for me to see
all the little unruly tongues
of his nose hairs sticking out—I don't

recognize him at first,
striding through the world all alone like that
as if he weren't my dentist, as if

he didn't belong in my dentist's office,
as if he had a life outside
my head. That's when he tilts his head

and looks at me askance as if
I were sitting there in his dentist's chair,
and then he gives me a smile that says

he not only recognizes me,
but he recognizes himself inside
my head, where I've been keeping him

prisoner. And he raises a deft hand
and lets himself out
with a wave.

Repair

My wife's ex is up on the roof
repointing our chimney.
I can hear him walking around up there

as I lie here in bed thinking
about the symbolism. It feels
a little like he's walking on my grave

and a little like I'm sleeping in his. "He's very
handy," said my wife. "He can fix
anything." I suppose most men

would find it too emasculating
to hire their wife's ex-husband
as a handyman. But I am not

most men. And I am not
the least bit handy. As for their marriage,
that was something he couldn't

fix, not after he cheated on her.
And now the bricks are flying
outside my window, bits of mortar

and flashing raining down as he chisels
them loose. My wife is getting
out of the shower. I can hear her

humming to herself in there. Soon
she will stroll into our bedroom with
a towel around her head, her magnificent

nipples shining and a grave
mischief in her eyes as she begins
making love to me all morning

beneath the hammering blows.

Worcester

In Worcester, Massachusetts,
outside the Worcester Free Public Library,
there's a line of homeless people
waiting to freshen up in the library's
free public toilets. And the senior librarian
isn't happy about it. How many will borrow a book
when they're done in the toilets? she asks the junior librarian
who is returning a book of poems by Elizabeth Bishop
to the poetry shelf. Before she moved to Worcester
for the junior librarian job, the junior librarian
lived with her aunt in Greencastle, Indiana,
and didn't even know how to pronounce Worcester.
As for the homeless people, they aren't
happy about it, either. Some are heroin addicts.
And some are mentally ill. And some are both.
And some are neither. And some are here illegally
and trying to acquire English by distilling it
from the airwaves and the signage. And they would all
rather be reading their own books on their own
toilets in their own homes. Nevertheless, they love
the motion-activated faucets with sensors in them
where they need only hold up their empty hands to receive
the generous wordless warm egalitarian water flowing
over their wrists and palms and backs of their hands
like a blessing. And all of them, every last one,
would pronounce Worcester perfectly,
as a sort of benign library fine, if asked.

Poem for Anybody

The first time anybody
put their tongue in my mouth
I was nonplussed, in-
coherent, grossed out.
I was also in love with this anybody,
it needs to be said, and all
I really wanted was their tongue
to say they loved me too.
This was many years ago when the spring
came sudden, warm and wet
as that tongue—and anybody
with any sense in their head
or blood in their veins
would have reciprocated in
kind. But I was as chaste
as the two-consecutive-cheeks
version of the French kiss,
terminally shy, and ignorant
as spit. All I really knew was
when anybody got that close
they got blurry. So I pushed
them away. Oh what I wouldn't
give to push rewind and pull
anybody close. Let anybody in.

The New Criticism

My stepdaughter
says I'm boring.
"Everything you say
is boring and like
so seventies." Her mother
says I'm wonderful, though.
"She's being fresh. Don't
listen to her," she says.
But I can't help listening
because I want to be
fresh and not boring,
and I want to say 'like'
like my stepdaughter
because everything
is like something, not
exactly but sort of.
And she's so contemporary
and provocative and like
alive. She knows all the new
neologisms and would
never use *neologism*
in a poem. Like ever.

Poem

Some pronounce it *poim*.
Like it has an *oy* inside it.
The way an oyster
has an *oy* inside it. The way
all poems ought to have
a little *oy veh*
and a little *oyez! oyez!*
inside them.

Others pronounce it *po-um*.
Like it has an *um* inside it.
A thoughtful pause.
A caesura. A possum
that got run over,
its esses elided.

Me, I always say *pome*.
Like an apple or pomme
I want to bite into
because it has an *om* inside it,
a mystic and sacred
syllable I can't wait to reach
and I have no patience
for all the diphthongs.

All of My Animals Are Old

The retriever sleeps all the time
in a corner, the cat drinks

all the time from the sink,
the hamster is blind and obese,

the rabbit just stares off into space,
chewing. Even the lion slinking

through my dreams is more
fearful than fearsome these days

and seems to be balding
from some nasty skin disease.

Only the Chihuahua (be still,
mi corazón) is restless as ever,

alert to every noise in the house,
jumpy sentry perched on my chest,

barking his false alarms.

My P.U.

Somebody, maybe Maria Callas, maybe
Sutherland, kept crooning, "*Mai piu, mai piu...*"
on the Welbilt radio in my grandmother's
living room. While somebody else, maybe
me, maybe my cousin Michael, had recently
farted. Never again would I hear that aria
(which was at least a hundred years old)
without hearing me and my cousin Michael
(who were at most eight and ten years old,
respectively) laughing hysterically and dying
operatically over and over again on the couch,
with that mortified diva confessing mournfully,
and that smell rising up as rich and sad as history.

Lost Sock

There is a dark side
to the dress socks
in the top drawer. They sort
according to some dark principle
of chaos and the estrangement
of identical twins—the precipitous
divorces of the happily married
are no less confounding
than these fine upstanding dress socks
you could once trust with your ankles
and your pedigree,
your onward and upward mobility,
suddenly turning against you
and each other
and themselves.
The motley characters you sometimes see
gathered around park benches,
passing the joint or the bottle,
are this kind of lost—
the transient attachments,
the fleeting allegiances
dissolving as soon as the spirits stop flowing,
each going his own way.

Sucky Poem

Because I suspect
that I suck.
Because I have suspected it
all this time.
Because I literally
sucked my thumb until I was
thirteen and a half,
shamefully, inexorably, clandestinely,
pretending to my parents
that I didn't anymore.
(My mother knew, though.
She knew.)
Because my bar mitzvah was a fraud, my father
kissing me on the cheek, saying,
"Now you are a man
in the eyes of God
and our people." Because our people
included my cousin Naomi from Brooklyn
with the long black hair and frank
mischief in her eyes.
And because it was the right thumb, never the left,
because I tried the left, of course, but it didn't
satisfy the way the right one did,
probably for reasons
anatomical. And finally,
because my parents are dead now
and I suspect that I suck
figuratively, having pretended
to myself all this time
I was great.

Feckless

It comes from the Scots *feck*,
which sounds like an f-bomb
though it isn't an f-bomb.
Though it may be a distant
cousin. Go ahead, say it: feck-
less. Feels good, doesn't it?
You could try it out at home.
Say it to your father: "Dad,
that is totally feckless." And if
he says to watch your language
and sends you to your room,
you can bet your effing
dictionary as soon as your back is turned
he'll be looking it up himself.
And you will have taught him something.
And you will have taught yourself
to use feckless to good effect.
Which is still really the only way
to make a new word your own.
You have to give it to people. Pick
their pockets and give it back
before anyone looks up.

Spring

There's too much sex in the world.
Just thinking about all the sex in the world
turns me off. There's too much increase.
Everywhere I look these days
there's fecundity. Everyone and everything
is prolific as fuck. It makes me feel
unproductive. It makes me feel downright
old. It wasn't always this way, though.
There wasn't always too much sex in the world,
and just thinking about all the sex in the world
used to turn me on. I used to love to watch
all the sex in the world. I was a collector
in my youth. When the Internet came along
I was a sort of researcher, searching again
and again, for all of the beautiful
bodies in the world, which never before
in the history of the world had been so
accessible. But now there's too much
access, too much sex, too much seed
on the wind, too much pollen in the air,
too much copulating on the ground. There's
too much begetting in the world and I'm getting
old. I'm getting downright chaste.

That Crying Thing

What is that
crying thing that I do
that isn't crying exactly,
more like a wave, a breaker
that doesn't break, doesn't
burst into tears
but just keeps swelling,
plunging toward the steep beach
at the back of my throat,
curving deliciously,
the crest thrusting forward,
the trough forming
that beautiful concave place
in which I could live
forever, just catching my breath
in the almost
but not quite spilling over,
that cherished, hollow space?

Deaf Bachelor Party

They've blindfolded one among them.
Now they're finger spelling in his hand
and marching him dizzy round Quincy Market
where our little crowd of onlookers has formed,
drawn to the sight of their uproarious
silence. We watch their sign language, try to follow.
Presumably he's the one who, hungover,
dies into marriage in the morning.
But tonight he's theirs, their sport, the ball
of banter flying from hand to hand,
and each hand seems to add a different twist,
a new and inscrutable spin to this game of catch,
the whips and throws of their signs as noiseless
as their laughter is loud. And it grows louder
as they guide him to the horse-and-carriage tours
at the curb, place his hand on a horse's ass
and watch his face for a sign: he feels around,
sniffs, tilts his head at a listening angle,
then signs some untranslatable pun that sends them
howling, boneless, weaving in wobbles and reels
till they've reached the solemn statue of Josiah Quincy.
They snap to attention, salute, park the bewildered
bridegroom face-front, guide his hand down the aquiline
marble nose, lips, chin, cravat, down to the inevitable
crotch! All hands on! Which cracks them up all over again
and even coaxes some titters from us, their emboldened
audience daring closer, having trailed them from horse
to statue to the doors of the pub they file into, leaving us
out. Which is where we were all along, we suddenly realize.
A few of us clap, then look down at our hands a moment
before thrusting them back in our pockets
where they seem to belong.

Visine

My left eye is killing me,
I say to my wife. It could be
allergies, she says. It could be
my retina getting ready
to detach, I say, or glaucoma
or syphilis or cancer. Why
do you always have to jump
to your death? she says.
I don't answer right away.
At the CVS, a whole aisle
of eye drops: drops for dry eyes,
drops for watery eyes, drops
for red and itchy eyes. My eyes
light on Visine and suddenly
I'm sixteen again and smoking
pot every day and trying to hide it
from my mother, cutting classes
left and right and writing
my stupid clever poems
about sex and trees and death.
There's a poem in here just itching
to get out, I think, as I tilt
my head back and squeeze:
two fat drops stinging as they go
to work. And how long before
Johnson & Johnson figured out
the reason for the precipitous jump
in sales? And how long before
I fell so far behind in high school
I ended up dropping out?

The truth is, I've been jumping
to my death all my life. Because
it's good practice, I say to my wife.
And what about your eye, is it
still killing you? she says. No, I say,
but now my feet hurt. And also
my right knee. That could be
from all the jumping, she says.

Lost Erections

I'll never forget that first one,
how we looked for it together
everywhere. Thinking

she was the one who lost it,
she apologized.
But it was mine to lose, I told her.

It's our loss, she said, ruefully
buttoning up
after doing yeoman's work

to try and find it. I never
saw her again and it remained
lost forever. Robert K. Merton

coined the phrase "self-fulfilling prophesy"
in 1948, ten years before
I was born: "The specious validity

of the self-fulfilling prophesy
perpetuates a reign of error,"
he wrote. Which explains why,

after losing that first one,
the fear of losing was hard to master.
In fact, it made a (write it!) disaster

of my sex life for decades after,
undermining every love poem
I ever wrote. "This could be

a love poem," says the attractive
elderly woman at the poetry workshop
where I am workshopping this poem.

"Perhaps what you need to focus on," she offers,
"is the balance between imagination
and didacticism, letting the latter

remain in the shadows,
letting the former
win out. Our poems

might one day teach us, the writers."

Bar Mitzvah Boy Considers the Lobsters in the Tank

I wonder if they suffer,
their claws tied up like that.
Like trying to yawn
with your elbows. Poor things,
I'd like to bust them out of there,
buy them up and let them all go
in the creek behind our house.
At $10.99 a pound,
and five dollars a week,
it would take me, let's see,
a pretty long time. That big one
climbing up on top of the others,
his foot in someone's eye—
what does it get him but closer
to the lobster pot? Better
to hide underneath or in back.
Be inconspicuous. Blend in.
Look out the window
like you're considering the weather:
tum-tee-tum. Even so,
they could call on you.
The world is like that.
But if you have the answer—
if you know your Torah portion
and your Haftarah portion
and all the songs and prayers—
you have nothing to fear. You can
sit anywhere. Hum a little tune.
Be conspicuous. Be idle. Be brazen.

When they call on you,
just start singing.
They'll praise you and maybe
give you enough money
to save all the lobsters.
Which would be a real mitzvah.

Elegy

All the lost time
spent looking
at the breasts of women

instead of the soft shapes
of clouds, the shoulders
of trees,

the jounce of a wave,
swell of the tide,

areolae
on a veined leaf
or insect's wing.

Diva

When he heard her sing he wanted
to make love to her. But then when
they were making love he wanted
her to sing. Because he was having
a little trouble, well, performing. Maybe
if she'd sing a little something it would
help him get in the mood—you know?

No, she didn't know. And she wouldn't
sing while having sex—that was just
too weird. And dressing quickly,
she asked him at the door, "What
do you think I am, a snake charmer?"
and scowled at his shrinking member,
which resembled a little cobra in a hood.

Lagomorph

Before she arrived
he had this philosophical look,
always chewing things over
while staring off into the distance
and masticating a piece of lettuce—
our pet rabbit, Pepper,
lop-eared, brindled, solitary
and liking it like that.

He wouldn't let anyone pick him up
except Amber, who was eight
and a half, and wanted another.
"To keep him company," she implored.
But we said no. If we get another
male they will fight. If we get a female
there will be lots of company
before long. Pepper looked

demurely off, sniffing the air as if
on the brink of an idea. In the end
we caved, keeping them apart
for the first few weeks in the easy-
to-assemble duplex hutch from
Petsmart. But Pepper grew
distracted. Her smell was more
than was dreamt of in his philosophy,

and he looked so miserable
and so horny
that Amber took it upon herself
to unlatch the dividing lintel and let them.

The relief was palpable, the silence
pregnant as they blinked lovingly up
from inside their cozy
two-bedroom apartment.

But soon she began to nip at him
and hiss. Her belly grew large
and her appetite grew voracious.
Pepper grew skeptical, fearful, old,
that distant look returning to his eyes
as though he were questioning
all of the assumptions
and all of the assertions
of a lifetime.

Arse Poetica

Before we could spell it
or use it in a sentence,
we had defined our own

aesthetic. We'd invented
a nomenclature,
raised the phenomenon
of farting

to the level of sport—
you might even say
to the level of art:

In only his underwear
and his glory, the reigning
champion would step
into the ring

of radiant 10-year-old faces, bow
to each of the four winds
and then to the ref,
who introduced the challenger,

who emerged from a circle
of fans chanting his name,
reaching out to touch
his diminutive butt,
all bets riding
on its famed eloquence.

Then each contestant
would grip his post,
knees bent slightly,
enough to simulate
but not stimulate
a movement,
which would disqualify—

control, as in any art,
meant the difference between
the blurting out of gross experience
and its transformation
into pure utterance.

But where are they now,
the contenders, the graduates
of that inelegant
Aeolian school?

Are they chemists, musicians,
proctologists, meteorologists,
their cheeks puffed out
with the music, the theory,
the prognostications?
And do they remember

when back in their pimples
they were full of hot air
and knew it, and made it
into something to get good at,
something to win at,
and to laugh at—God in heaven,
to laugh like that again!

Kazoo

When Lafferty asked to join the band
we asked him what instrument he played.
"Ka-zoo," he sneezed, smiling as big
as a small horn section. It was 1967, the British
Invasion was underway, and the sexual revolution
was in full swing. The submarine-shaped Kazoo
was being mass-produced by the Original
American Kazoo Company of Eden, New York,
but none of us had ever seen one before.
"Kazoo?" we asked in a rising iambic chorus.
"Kazoo," he echoed and it sounded vaguely
like "Shazam!" as he suddenly fished it out
of his shirt pocket with a flourish, smiling as wide
as a conjurer holding it up for our inspection.
"What is it? It looks like a toy. Is this some kind of
joke?" We were a serious rock band after all.
"Give me the mike," he said, rubbing his hands,
the smile gone now. So we plugged him in
and he started to wail: a cross between a tenor sax
and a swarm of bees. Man, the kid was good.
He was better than good. He was virtuosic. He had
the line and he had the rhythm and he blew
us all away as one by one we joined in and started
to jam. But it was right then, in that moment when
he saw it written on our faces—that he was just
what we needed to be great—that he stopped playing,
resubmerged that submarine into the shallows
of his breast pocket, dropped periscope, raised
anchor, and on his way out, fired one torpedo:
"I quit," he said before we could ask him to join.

Benedict Arnold

"I did my report on Benedict Arnold
because those other guys were all taken
by the time I got home from my grandfather's
funeral in Florida. George Washington
and Thomas Jefferson and Benjamin Franklin
and Alexander Hamilton and John
Hancock and John Adams and John Jay,
et al., were all taken and only Benedict
Arnold remained. Because nobody likes a traitor.
And his name is synonymous with betrayal.
The most infamous turncoat in our history.
But he makes for an interesting story.
And isn't that what history ought to be?
I mean, think for a minute about what the man
risked. The punishment for high treason
for much of the history of England and its colonies
was emasculation, evisceration, and decapitation,
in that order. In other words, they would cut off
your weenie (excuse me, Mrs. Cunningham,
but it's true, you can Google it if you want to),
then slice you open, and after you had finished
watching your intestines spill onto the ground,
they would cut off your head for good measure,
stick it on a spike or palisade, and there among
the other traitorous heads display it for weeks
or months at a time. For reasons of public decency
women convicted of high treason were usually
burnt at the stake instead. And that concludes
my report on Benedict Arnold. Any questions?"

Desiderata

Don't be an asshole
if you can help it.
But if you can't help it, help
others to understand the asshole.
Be an ambassador for assholes.
Carry the whole rootless and diffuse
assholic diaspora in your heart
as you go forth into the world
trying not to be an asshole
and failing ineluctably.
Because you can't be
what you want to be if
you can't be what you are first.
So go ahead, be that way.
Be an asshole but also be
amazed and heartbroken
and sick with desire for the world
and all of its beautiful
ineluctable assholes.
Be their apologist, their poet—
let their feeling gather in you
like a wind. Sing, asshole,
the anger of assholes.
Sing the epic assholery
and douchebaggery
of the dull and the ignorant,
of the helplessly intelligent,
of the mean and unworthy,
the self-righteous and wholly dickhead.

Sing their ignominy, their abject luck
and grim astonishment. But also,
asshole, sing the shocked grace that comes,
unaccountably, of loving them.

Arata

We loved and hated Mr. Arata,
our soccer coach in junior high.
He yelled at us a lot because
he loved soccer and hated
to lose. We were fourteen and he was
married. I wondered if he loved
his wife and yelled at her too.
I can still see her standing there
at the edge of our soccer field,
worrying her hands and wincing
as he yelled at us for ducking
when we should have headed the ball,
yelled at us for passing when
we should have taken a shot,
yelled at us for shooting when
we should have passed.
He yelled at us so much he lost
his voice. After that, he used
a megaphone. We were seven
and seven when I stood up
for something more important
than winning: namely, seeing
that there was another way,
a quiet, leaf-strewn way that led
off the soccer field altogether, past
Mrs. Arata wringing her hands,
and down into the adjacent woods
where the courtships of small animals
were going on in the ravines. I used
my head—I used my feet—I quit
outright and never looked back.

To this day I am uncomfortable
around people who love sports
and hate losing. I love a good game
as much as the next guy. But I hate
the next guy when he starts yelling
at his beloved team.

Backstory

If you were here I would tell you
how I threw my back out
and everyone I talked to, I mean everyone,
had a backstory—
an uncle or cousin or coworker
or husband or friend of a friend with a bad
back that got better at the chiropractor's
or the physical therapist's or under
the knife. I couldn't stand up straight
for two weeks. And as much as that hurt—
and it hurt a lot, let me tell you—
having to listen to everyone and his brother's
backstory hurt even worse. Because I didn't
care. I mean I really didn't. "Maybe if I didn't
care, it wouldn't hurt so much," I remember
you saying back when you were here. I wish
you were still here. I think
not caring hurts as much as caring.
In fact, I think it hurts even worse.

Backstops

The backstops are flying away,
the ones our great-grandfathers built,
the ones we climbed when we were small,
perching on top of their huge overhangs
and looking out over the baseball fields of life
like so many birds riding the old and rusty
rhinoceroses, which seemed not to move at all—
that's how slow they were moving—
while we sat there munching our lunches
and watching the games. And who
would have thought the backstops would ever
not be there, standing behind us and our
children and our children's children
when the time came to step up to the plate
and take a few good swings? But look—
the backstops are flying away, they're flying
out of the park, flying out of town, flying out of
the country to other countries far away,
and what can the umpires do but remove their masks
and squint in disbelief like the rest of us
at the backstops going, going, going, gone.

Erica

Once upon a time I loved Erica.
I loved her name almost as much
as I loved Erica. She was tall
and athletic and had a distinctly
masculine way of walking
down the hall, holding her books
like a discus at her thigh the way
boys do, rather than an armful
of flowers at her chest like all
the girls. But it was the boyish ring
of her name, which comes from
Eric—though you didn't hear
the Eric in Erica until you saw it—
that really put the Erica in erotica.

Commodity

So my friend Bob asks me how the poetry's going.
Bob who doesn't write poetry but is good with people
and good at asking you questions about yourself
and saying your name after every sentence, like a refrain,
and looking you in the eye while you look at his shoes.
And he's good at making money. If you ask him how
he's doing, he says he's doing *excellent.* He's that kind
of annoying. So he asks me how the poetry's going
and I tell him good, excellent. I tell him I got one in *Poetry,*
a real coup, and one in the *Missouri Review* and two
in *Shenandoah.* Plus a whole bunch more I haven't sold
that I'm sending out again. He raises an eyebrow, says
to hear me talk you'd think the poem was a commodity.
And I look down at his beautiful shoes. Because it's the truth.

Universal Studios, Orlando

I'm sitting out all the rides
because they make me dizzy,
reading a book of poems
here in the shadow of The Hulk
while my wife and stepkids
fly through the air with the greatest of ease,
screaming. My favorite part
is the rain. How it comes on
suddenly, lasts only briefly, leaves
a faint scent of itself in the air like a good
haiku. My stepdaughter Amber,
finding me here in the shade,
says she feels sorry for me—
"sitting there all alone with your book
and missing out on all the fun."
She takes me by the hand, leads me
over my objections to Dr. Seuss's
Trolley Train Ride, a little choo-choo
with poems on the walls that rhyme.
"This is more your speed," she says,
sitting down beside me, my knees
coming up to my chin, the strapping
attendant with tats and a flip grin
buckling us in.

Conductor

He accompanies himself
on his silver hole-punch,
singing *Tickets Please*
and walking famously
down the aisle, another
audience in the next car,
and the next. I want to be
like him. I want to sing
All Aboard! I want to wear
a serious hat and a change
machine. I want to carry
a wad of cash and take it
out often. He is fluent in
the rhythm of the train. He
could be dancing. I could be
dancing with him. He leads
with his hand on my seatback,
his hip brushing my shoulder
as he clicks past, singing
and dancing and playing
an instrument. And no one
claps. Because they're all
reading or texting or just
looking out the window
at all the passing lives
they will never enter.

Deaf and Dumb

The Deaf man in the waiting room
asks me how long I've been working
as an interpreter. I tell him
many years. "Awesome," he says.
We sit there chatting, waiting
for the doctor to come.

He tells me a little about himself.
His parents and grandparents are Deaf.
His siblings are Deaf. His two young children
are fourth generation Deaf. The hereditary
master status of a kind of Deaf aristocracy
in the Deaf world. And I am duly
impressed. My turn to say, "Awesome."

He is getting his Ph.D. in sociolinguistics.
His signing is graceful, fluid, symphonic—
like water everywhere seeking its own
level. Chatting him up in the waiting room
is a pure joy, one of the perks
of my profession.

But the doctor is dumb about Deaf people.
In the little examining room
he doesn't address the Deaf man directly
but tells me to "tell him" this, "ask him" that.
The Deaf man notices, tells the doctor
to tell him himself, in the second person.
But the doctor doesn't know what the second person is.

He examines the Deaf man but he doesn't
see him. He doesn't look in his eyes.

He says to say "Ahh," but the Deaf man
refuses to vocalize, mouth wide open,
fists forming at his sides, uvula
hanging there like a punching bag,
silent and motionless,
while we wait.

Ode on a Treadmill

Not the proverbial treadmill
that conjures up hamsters and mice
and us in our circular
narratives. But this new
or almost new NordicTrack
that I got for fifty bucks
from Lori Novak because
it had turned into a coat rack
and she didn't want it anymore.
I have installed it in a corner
of my basement where I walk
every morning and every evening
for thirty minutes at a good clip.
And I love it, I love it, I have fallen
back in love with walking—
I haven't felt this way since
I was sixteen or seventeen
months old: elated, exhilarated,
intoxicated to be bipedal.
Putting one foot in front of the other
somehow turned into an idiom
not long after I learned how—
it turned into words the way
the whole world turned into words
as I grew literate, literary, sedentary,
fat. But now I'm breaking a sweat,
walking around the world
in a corner. And lo, the world
is growing real again. And I am
growing younger and younger

and younger, up here on the bridge
of my time machine, the console
flashing all these rosy numbers—
distance, velocity, vital signs—
as I go striding, gliding,
tottering, toddling
shakily off my starship
and into the shower.

Lion

The gazelles
speed by in their
huge metallic herds
on both sides
of the highway.
The solitary
powerful nomad
hunting them
with his radar gun
crouches behind
some trees in the median.
Out of the corner
of her eye she sees him
too late—his eyes
already flashing
in her rearview,
her heart leaping
like an antelope
pronking in her chest
as she flees among
the other antelope,
hoping it isn't her
he will outrun, over-
take, pull over
the rumble strip
to the shoulder,
his grille breathing
hot on her tail lights,
taking his time
writing her up,
her doe-eyed
hazards blinking.

Nothing

He had nothing to say, he said,
adding only that saying so
was in itself finally beautiful and true.

That was his message. It was
something no one else had ever said
quite the way he was saying it.

Many thought they heard a quiet
sort of unexceptional wisdom in it
and nodded their heads in agreement,

nodded their heads to the music of it,
which wasn't an easy music per se,
not the kind you'd get up and dance to,

or beat a drum to, or hum to yourself
in an abstracted sort of way. But it grew
louder. So when his enemies and detractors

tried to silence him, they couldn't silence him.
Because he had nothing to say.
They could only scratch their heads and listen.

Privilege

Take, for example, the grass
in the suburbs of America,
how it forecloses the likes of
curly dock, tansy, clover,
creeping thyme,
buttercup, ragweed—
any raggedy brown
or blue or red or yellow
unruly thing
applying for entry here,
hoping to live and to flourish here—
all the so-called weeds,
all the beautiful wildflowers—
turned away, mowed down,
poisoned. And hasn't it always
been this way, only the pure,
cropped, decorous green
grass and its offspring welcomed here?
But at what cost to all of us
this skewed sense of beauty
and propriety, this monochrome
monoculture with its monotonous
traditions of separateness
and supremacy, totally lacking
in any flavor or utility
or spirit? The dispirited grass,
asleep in its vast bed
of privilege, dreams of the invading
hordes of color, riots
of dandelion, chicory, purslane,
which all make fine eating
and live on the other side,

out in the waste places,
out along the roadsides,
not very far away
but far enough away
so that the lonely, privileged,
uninflected grass begins to feel
a profound sense of loss
and a profound sense of sadness
to think of the fine company
and the fine eating
of its despised neighbors,
all the brothers and sisters
whom it has never met
and does not know at all.

Student Driver

I hate this stalled poem
which has gotten only as far
as the title
written in big letters
on the little billboard
bolted to the roof of the car in front of me,
the two shadowy figures
in the front seat
putting their heads together
over the trundling dumb
progress of this poem.
I'm in a hurry.
But the poem is going nowhere and I really
want to help them with it,
because I think I can see
how if they take the next off-ramp
it will be the perfect ending:
happy, easy, clever. But no,
the poem wants to go
somewhere else. It wants to go
where I am going.
And what can I do but
stare straight ahead
at the two heads in the front seat,
while the poem looks back
at the two heads in the front seat
of a different car, an older car,
a rusty green Dodge Dart
on a quiet, dusty backstreet
in a time and place before
seat belts were invented—

one head small, curly, mine,
the other larger, heavier, graying,
leaning under the weight of all
that love, all that history,
careful not to condescend
as it leans down, as it leans
lovingly in, beginning to instruct,
describe, praise, delight, and ending
in wisdom.

Guilt at the Transfer Station

There's a lot of baggage
in the garbage
at the transfer station,
which we used to call
the dump. Someone is throwing out
all these old suitcases,
a mattress and a box spring,
a bunch of cardboard boxes
which the recycling lady is saying
are a violation: "They should be
broken down and recycled."
In the backseat of my car
three large black plastic bags
bulge guiltily, a small slit
divulging a suspicious-looking
refulgence. Black like a thief's
black woolen cap pulled down
over the shining evil faces
of my old television, old computer,
and several small appliances.
Cathode ray tubes which will take
a hundred thousand years
to biodegrade. In the ninth century
when the Danish nose tax was imposed,
delinquent taxpayers were punished
by having their noses slit.
But I'll be damned if I'm going to pay
the CRT recycling fee
just to throw out my old computer and TV,
especially after paying through the nose

for my new ones. And the stink
of the unfairness of it all rises
as I lower my bags over the edge
of the world, the slit ripping open to reveal
a gaping, luminous gash.

Bard

Once upon a time in a small
college for creative fuck-ups
on the Hudson, there was what you would call
a sophomoric English major
living in a room in Albee Hall
with a wall of bay windows opening
onto the quad. As an English major,
he would have said his room communicated
onto the quad, knowing as he did
the various senses of *communicate,*
and being at that time what he would call
a communicant in the church of rock & roll
with a formidable record collection
and a formidable stereo
with four formidable speakers communicating
what he would have called his sense of self,
his sense of meaning and meaninglessness
and truth and beauty and anarchy—
broadcasting it through those open bay windows
at top volume onto the quad
at all hours. So whenever a fusty old Shakespeare
scholar or faculty member or bespectacled
administrator passed beneath Albee Hall,
he or she would invariably look up
and make what you would call
a face, a scowl of the purest contempt
and disgust, as though what emanated there
from those open bay windows were a communicable
disease. Of which there were, it should be said,
one or two going around in that small
college for creative fuck-ups
rock & rolling on the Hudson.

Riffing on Rilke

That was the summer I stayed up in Annandale
in a big old Victorian house off-campus,
smoking weed and translating Rilke
up on the roof. It was an independent
study and I got two credits for ten Elegies.
I got really tan up there too. I got the weed
from the bass player who lived in the basement apartment.
We'd smoke a bone and have the creative
juices flowing by breakfast. Then I'd climb
out on the roof with my Coppertone and dictionary
while he got down with his jazz in the basement
where it was cool. And we'd improvise till sundown,
his funky bass line buzzing up through the bones
of that creepy old castle, me straddling the peak
of the roof, which felt like the nape of some enormous angel,
the pitched slopes like great forbidding wings
beginning to unfurl beneath my thighs
as I turned the pages of my Langenscheidt,
searching for just the right words in English
to capture the terrible beauty of the celestial hierarchy.
The more stoned I got the closer I felt I was getting
to Rilke's mystical vision, climbing higher
and farther along the hot roof tiles, nothing
but a diminishing joint between my lips for a balancing pole,
over the north gable to the very nose of the angel—
the dormer jutting out from the adjacent slope—
which I bestrode with the easy grace of a born horseman,
taking up the reins and flicking the orphaned roach
into the empty spaces below, perhaps that the birds
might feel the expanded air with more intimate flight.

Voyeur

Maybe if I did the opposite
it would yield a better result,
I remember thinking to myself
back when my best thinking

was getting me in a lot of trouble
and my best brushing
was getting me a lot of cavities.
Just do the opposite

of whatever it occurs to you to do
in any given situation. This seemed
a good strategy, especially to one who
always seemed to be getting it wrong.

So instead of brushing my teeth
I ate a candy bar every night
before going to bed. And another one
each morning before school.

"What's taking you so long?"
my mother called outside the bathroom
because it takes longer to eat a candy bar
than to brush your teeth. I'll bet you

didn't know that. There are lots of things
you can learn by doing the opposite.
Instead of studying for your science test
(which only ever got you Cs and Ds)

you can turn off the lights and gaze outside
your bedroom window. And you can see
into your neighbor's bedroom window
in the house opposite, without her seeing you—

and you learn a thing or two
about light and dark, and girls' undergarments, and what
lies under them. Doing the opposite was really
paying off. Until I got the abscess, then the F

in science class. Then my parents got that phone call
from the neighbors, accusing me of something
that sounded kind of French. Which is how
I learned a new word from doing it.

Shy

Mick Jagger is shy.
I read that in *Rolling Stone.*
On stage he's all swagger and tongue
and *oh yeah oh yeah oh yeah*
and *baby, come on!*
And man, the guy can scream
very grittily and in tune.
But offstage he's a kitten,
says Keith, who's known him
since they were seven
or eight. And a gentleman,
say the scores of women
he was too shy or polite
to hit on outright, so they had to
jump his bones just to get things
rolling. But once they got rolling
he could hold his own with the best of them.
Which reminds me a little of myself.
I have a rock & roll star inside me
that I'm mostly too shy
to let out. But when it's just me
and the Stones all alone in my car,
Mick's syncopated screaming
mixing it up with Keith's inexorable guitar rhythms—
it starts me up. And then I'm
rolling down the highway doing 80,
gyrating in the driver's seat,
screaming grittily and in tune,
my eyes and mouth fully dilated,
my shyness behind me,
splayed and bloody
in the rearview.

A Modest Proposal

The men cannot be trusted with their penises.
We must take the penises out of the hands
of the men, and put them into the competent,
containing, restraining hands of the state. It's as
plain as the noses on the faces that the penises
have been running amok ever since it was first
given to men to handle them. Just ask the women.
Ask the women and also ask the children
how many times and how many ways
and in how many places the penises have offended.
The evidence is before us. And behind us.
It goes all the way back through time to the first
penis, to God's penis, which no one ever talks about
either. Because it got deleted, expurgated, cut
from the canon. Which is why it's the elephant
in the room's penis. It's the elephant's penis
in the room. It's the biggest, most culpable,
most unrepentant penis ever and we never ever
talk about it. Let's talk about it. Let's expostulate!
Let's remonstrate! Regulate the penises! Legislate
the penises! All the penises, including the state's
own penis, and the church's penis, too, which technically
and theologically isn't the same as God's penis,
which is omnipresent, omnipotent, rapture-
ready. Though for all practical and profane purposes
they are one and the same penis. The Penis is one.

Man Begging Outside the Dunkin' Donuts

"I gave on the way in,"
I tell him on my way out.
He's holding the door open
for me and the other haves
like a doorman or a maraca player
playing his half-empty cup
of coins. "Thank you," he says,
"I remember you." And I feel
remembered, exonerated,
philanthropic, until he says,
"But nothing says you can't
give again, boss." Then I feel
exploited, indignant, misanthropic,
and I walk huffily past him with
my overflowing cup of resentment.
He gets you coming and going.
Get a job, I want to yell at him.
But this *is* his job. He's always
here. Every single morning
like clockwork. He never misses
a shift. He's on his feet all day
dealing with a public that
despises him and his tin cup's
tintinnabulation, a music as old
as the oldest profession in the world.
"Good morning," he sings to every
half-awake, scowling, disdainful,
gainfully employed soul that passes
through the door. And it's more
than you or I could muster any
given morning. It's giving all to all.

Only Child

In my one and only childhood
I didn't like to eat in front of people.
I think I thought it made me look weak.
I think I thought I ought to be immune
to hunger and thirst, and rain and cold.
I refused to carry an umbrella
or wear a jacket or a hat. I think
I thought that having a body was
something to deny, or deplore,
or indulge in only secretly and
alone. I don't know why I thought that.
I sucked my thumb surreptitiously
until I was thirteen and a half,
pretending to my father that I didn't.
My mother knew, though.
Years later, the mother of my children
wanted a divorce. "Because you're
weak," she said. And what
could I say to that? After all, I'd been
eating in front of people for years,
carrying an umbrella and wearing
a jacket and a hat. All of a sudden,
I found myself alone and right all along.
I was right all along, I said to myself,
curled up in that narrow motel bed,
separated from my wife and kids, my thumb
tasting like it belonged to somebody else.

Pancreatic Answer

When she asks you to write a poem
about *her*, because you're spending so much time
agonizing over the poems you write
about everyone else and everything else in the world,
and your anniversary is coming up,
and maybe just for once you could shower
the woman you love with a little attention
by agonizing over her for a change—
here's what you do: start by writing about the agony
of waiting for her reply, all those years ago,
when you first told her exactly how you felt
about her mouth, its shape, its sheer
perfection. Then write about the joy
of grazing on that mouth ever since
and never being filled. Write about
the agony of seeing her cry, how when she's sad
it makes you more unhappy than any
unhappiness of your own. Frame it
like that: your happiness on the one hand,
your sadness on the other, put it in a box
and give it to her as an anniversary present
and maybe it will be exactly what she wants.
And maybe not. Maybe she'll object to the third person,
saying it's distant and ironic, exactly the way
you are when you fight. And maybe she'll dislike
the artifice, the frank mischief and mischievous
frankness, and just the whole convoluted
serious joke of the poem. And what if she doesn't get it?
What if she doesn't understand the poem at all?
Understanding is overrated, you must say in the poem,
the way understanding the function of your pancreas

when you're dying of pancreatic cancer is overrated.
The way understanding fossil fuels and fracking
and the effects of fluctuating commodity markets
on the price of gasoline when the world is dying
from the inside out is overrated. We're alive and we are
dying (you say in the poem, so now the poem is
cooking with gas) and I love you here and now and don't
understand any of it, any of it, at all. And that's okay.
It's perfectly beautifully utterly overwhelmingly okay.

History of Love

Because he loves the way she has
of touching him
and because she loves the way he has
of loving her
each has learned the other's
way and the other's touch
so when love turns
and the world turns
and the lovers turn from each other and go
to other lovers they take
they take all they know
of love and of touch
and they give it to another
and in this way love grows rich
and wise and wide among us
and in this way we are also
loving those who will come after
and those who came before
we ever came to love

Explication of Beauty

You want beauty
to want you. That's
what you really want.
You don't want beauty
for yourself. And you don't
want beauty for itself—
What you want is
to be wanted by beauty,
as though beauty were
wanting without you.
Which, of course, it is.
Beauty is wanting
without you. But you
don't see that yourself.
You don't see yourself
as completing beauty,
you who are completely
beautiful already.
Beauty holds you
wherever you see it.
And yet you want it
to want you. But you see
it doesn't want you.
And that makes you
inexplicably sad.

Cleaning the Rabbit Cage

The round, brown, uniform, odorless turds
like diminutive canon balls piled
in a tidy corner

are identically unidentical,
no two exactly alike,
like snowflakes. I'm shoveling them

into the urine-soaked newspaper,
examining one and then another
between my thumb and forefinger:

individual, fungible, fudgy,
yet in the aggregate
a perfect whole, a dusting,

a few errant pellets spilling
onto the floor as I gingerly
remove the mother lode.

And what must he think, Pepper,
masticating in the opposite
corner, knowing enough not to

shit where he eats, even in such close
quarters? What must he be thinking,
he who always seems to be thinking,

chewing things over and over
with his two sets of incisors,
one behind the other,

seeming to pay me no mind,
yet surely noticing me here,
my head inside his cage,

harvesting his excrement,
as though I had a mind
to make something out of it?

NatPoMo

So you want the poem to teach you something,
don't you? So listen up,
if you're ever in downtown Boston
needing to go, and there are no public restrooms,
head to the Massachusetts Eye and Ear Infirmary
on Charles Street, where up on the sixth floor
just outside of refractive surgery
and down the hall from vestibular diagnostics,
there's a one-seater big enough for someone in a wheelchair
to comfortably do what I did when I was in there,
which was first to take off my jacket,
because it was jacket weather—the beginning
of April, National Poetry Month—
and hang it on a hook behind the door
that locked with a reassuring *click,*
which rhymes with *hic,*
which is Latin for "here"
as in the phrase *hic jacet,* which means "here lies,"
which is what they write on tombstones—
and in that bathroom the size of a mausoleum for a small king
I sealed myself in and removed my jacket
and pants and underpants, sitting myself down
for a long period of time. An era. A whole dynasty
of OCCUPIED, just thinking about
whatever came to mind, the many-colored thoughts
flitting in and out like finches, like Darwin's finches
on the smallest island of the Galapagos
and *hic jacet* and sarcophagi and NatPoMo and refractive vestibules
and upright burials and upright pianos
and certain memorable lines from certain memorable poems
and what an apposite epitaph might be for me

when the time comes to leave this place, which could be
sooner than I know. Then I shifted a little, my belt buckle
clinking against my shoe, my colon whispering affirmations
to my rectum, and I took out my indelible pen
and graffitied these words on the wall: "Here sits
one who lies in service of the emotional truths."
I wrote it as a kind of You Are Here
for you. And for me, too.

Poetry & Rain

People who love poetry are like people who love the rain. We're in the minority. Most people hate rain. They look out their rain-streaked windows and scowl as though faced with a long and difficult poem. They blink beneath their umbrellas and shrug as though under the penumbra of an inscrutable poem. And sometimes it isn't raining exactly, but sort of misting, or sleeting, or spitting. It's kind of like that with poetry. Not exactly but sort of.

But the earth needs poetry as much as it needs rain. Even people who hate poetry and rain will grudgingly, grumblingly, admit this meteorological fact. They would just prefer that the poetry and the rain occur someplace else, someplace where the people who love poetry and rain can dance around and exult in it and the rest of us can take it in in smaller doses, in bottles or, preferably, teaspoons.

And then there is the smell of the rain, which is not unlike the smell of the poem. The smell of the rain before the rain is practically a poem itself. And the smell of the rain after the rain is reminiscent of poems about poems. There are poets who never write poems about poems and would just as soon not have to read them, either. They are like the people who come in out of the rain and fold up their umbrellas and briskly wipe off their shoulders and arms and sit back down to the task at hand. But then there are poets who love poems about poems. They write them often and love to read them. And they are like the people who come in out of the rain and their shoes are filled with the noise of it, and they do a little dance and give a little shout, and then they leave their umbrellas open to dry on the floor like big, black, articulated flowers which the cat eyes from a distance and is soon emboldened to approach and sniff and sit beneath and contemplate and lick.

Hell is having nothing to read but your own poems. Which is like having nothing to drink but your own bathwater. Or like carrying around your own urine sample for days or weeks at a time. Which is why we need each other's poems. We really do. But the thing is, poets can be very annoying people. We really can. As tiresome as rain. In fact, if not for the poetry, I don't think I'd have anything to do with us. And as for the poems, well, I think I could do without ninety percent of them. If not for the ten percent that I love, I don't think I'd have anything to do with poetry.

Happiness

The dog isn't happy
unless his head is
sticking out the car window.

The man isn't happy
unless his head is
happy.

The man and the dog
have this in common,
thinks the man,

driving around with the dog
in the backseat, nose
in the wind, happiness

in the air.

Revision

There used to be
a live chicken
in this poem.

There was a mountain
and a sailboat.
The Pacific Ocean

sloshing between stanzas.
And me like Adam
saying *Here am I*

to God who was also
near.

Acknowledgments

Thanks to the following magazines and websites, where many of these poems, often in earlier versions, originally appeared:

Asinine: "Happiness"
Blue Hour: "My P.U."
California State Literary Review: "Commodity"
Connecticut River Review: "Man Begging Outside the Dunkin Donuts"
Descant: "Poem"
Five-Two: Poetry on Crime: "Guilt at the Transfer Station"
Green Linden: "Deaf Bachelor Party"
The High Window: "Kazoo"
Ibbetson Street: "Bar Mitzvah Boy Considers the Lobsters in the Tank"
Kentucky Review: "One Ambition," "Out of Place," "Student Driver"
Leaping Clear: "That Crying Thing," "Backstory"
Lilliput Review: "Revision"
Mad Swirl: "Visine"
Mixitini Matrix: "Voyeur"
Off the Coast: "Spring," "The Calculus," "Worcester"
Poets Online: "Deaf and Dumb," "Riffing on Rilke"
Right Hand Pointing: "Backstops"
Seems: "The New Criticism," "Feckless," "Nothing," "A Modest Proposal"
Slant: "Lagomorph"
South Florida Poetry Journal: "Sucky Poem," "If Only Life Were Like Language"
Spillway: "Repair"
Sport Literate: "Arata"
Steam Ticket: "Only Child"
Straight Forward: "Poetry & Rain"
THAT Literary Review: "Pancreatic Answer," "Privilege"
Third Wednesday: "All of My Animals Are Old," "Arse Poetica," "Shy"
Your Daily Poem: "Ode on a Treadmill," "Lion"

About FutureCycle Press

FutureCycle Press is dedicated to publishing lasting English-language poetry books, chapbooks, and anthologies in both print-on-demand and ebook formats. Founded in 2007 by long-time independent editor/publishers and partners Diane Kistner and Robert S. King, the press incorporated as a nonprofit in 2012. A number of our editors are distinguished poets and writers in their own right, and we have been actively involved in the small press movement going back to the early seventies.

The FutureCycle Poetry Book Prize and honorarium is awarded annually for the best full-length volume of poetry we publish in a calendar year. Introduced in 2013, our Good Works projects are anthologies devoted to issues of universal significance, with all proceeds donated to a related worthy cause. Our Selected Poems series highlights contemporary poets with a substantial body of work to their credit; with this series we strive to resurrect work that has had limited distribution and is now out of print.

We are dedicated to giving all of the authors we publish the care their work deserves, making our catalog of titles the most diverse and distinguished it can be, and paying forward any earnings to fund more great books.

We've learned a few things about independent publishing over the years. We've also evolved a unique, resilient publishing model that allows us to focus mainly on vetting and preserving for posterity the most books of exceptional quality without becoming overwhelmed with bookkeeping and mailing, fundraising activities, or taxing editorial and production "bubbles." To find out more about what we are doing, come see us at www.futurecycle.org.

The FutureCycle Poetry Book Prize

All full-length volumes of poetry published by FutureCycle Press in a given calendar year are considered for the annual FutureCycle Poetry Book Prize. This allows us to consider each submission on its own merits, outside of the context of a contest. Too, the judges see the finished book, which will have benefitted from the beautiful book design and strong editorial gloss we are famous for.

The book ranked the best in judging is announced as the prize-winner in the subsequent year. There is no fixed monetary award; instead, the winning poet receives an honorarium of 20% of the total net royalties from all poetry books and chapbooks the press sold online in the year the winning book was published. The winner is also accorded the honor of being on the panel of judges for the next year's competition; all judges receive copies of all contending books to keep for their personal library.

Made in the USA
Monee, IL
31 October 2020

46457149R00049